ADDRESS

TO THE

FIRST GRADUATING CLASS

OF

Rutgers Female College;

DELIVERED IN

THE FOURTH AVENUE PRESBYTERIAN CHURCH.
(REV. DR. CROSBY'S),

ON

SABBATH EVENING, JUNE 2D, 1867.

BY

HENRY M. PIERCE, LL.D.,
PRESIDENT OF THE COLLEGE.

PUBLISHED BY REQUEST OF THE TRUSTEES.

New York:
AGATHYNIAN PRESS.

1867.

PRESIDENT'S ADDRESS.

In the year 1839, with great labor, care, expense, and after long consultation, was the Rutgers Female Institute founded. It grew out of an increasing sense of the importance of the duties of women, and of the need that her work should be well done. Hence the establishment of the school, with its course of studies, its libraries, its apparatus, its teachers. A quarter of a century has witnessed a great change in the education of woman; and the position of Rutgers Institute to-day, as a College, marks the character and degree of that change.

It has been my custom, to make a personal address to the members of each graduating class, as they have gone forth from the quiet of the school to the busy walks of life. My heart now impels me to follow this usage, but the change that has taken place in this institution, during the past year, seems to make appropriate to the present occasion, a few preliminary statements of my views as to what is the true position of woman, and what should be her education.

These are questions that deeply agitate the public mind. They are, in fact, the leading questions of the day; but in regard to them, I shall not shrink from the utterance of my opinions. Underlying the question of the education of woman, is the question of her equality with man; for if woman be inferior to man, so should be her education.

Some might be disposed to reverse this proposition, and

to say that just in proportion to her inferiority, should her training be more careful and complete. There might seem to be some truth in this idea; but a little deeper thinking will convince us that to try to make up in this way for her supposed deficiency, would be to attempt an impossibility. The end could not be reached; the bounds that nature had appointed could not be passed.

It is also clear that if woman be the equal of man, she should receive as good an education as man, a proposition too plain for argument. So is also our third proposition—which exhausts this branch of the subject—that if woman be superior to man, she should receive a better education than man: for it is a first principle in morals, that every power which God gave, He meant should be unfolded to its fullest extent.

I am fully persuaded that the time is not far distant, when it will be thought almost incredible that the question of the inferiority of woman should ever have been seriously debated. For it is not without higher warrant than that of human reason, that I would claim for woman an equal place by the side of man. When in the beginning God created the heavens, the earth, the sea, and all that in them is, even as He then made laws for the stars and the seas, so did He then fix and determine forever the sphere and the destiny of man and of woman. Driven out of Paradise into the world on account of sin, neither man nor woman took their place at once; and in the nature of the case, woman's sphere was the last of the two to be understood.

The Old Testament contains the germs of the great truths of all time; but over four thousand years were needed to prepare the human mind for the coming of Christ; and it was reserved for Christ fully to declare what place the Creator had designed for woman. I am fully persuaded that upon all great questions touching humanity, the human mind will at length accept the teachings of Christ as final; and the question whether or not woman is the equal of man, I conceive to be authoritatively settled by Him, when he pronounces marriage such a union as excludes the idea that there can be essential inferiority in one of the parties. His ideal of marriage, unknown alike to the classical nations and to the Hebrews, is incompatible with the inequality of the sexes. Nor do we find a trace in His life or teachings, or in those of His Apostles, which tends in the least to countenance such an idea. The few apparent exceptions to this statement grow out of Oriental usage, or are explained by the truth that subordination is consistent with equality. Not even superficial reasoners should have been misled by these exceptions, when, generally speaking, there is no distinction in the moral duties enjoined on each, none in the warnings and promises addressed to each, none at the cross, none in the day of judgment.

Equality, though it excludes the idea of inferiority, is consistent with diversity. There is a difference between the sexes, that at once raises the question whether there should not be a difference in their education.

After the most careful thought that I could give to the subject, I am of the opinion that it should be the same to a much greater extent than most persons are willing to concede. Up to a certain point, the education of men is much the same: beyond that point comes in a special training. Thus, on leaving college, the young man who is to pursue law, receives a legal training. But the great fact here to be noticed is, that up to a certain point, all liberally educated men are trained much in the same manner. For a long time, a liberal education seems to take no note of the specific ends, which finally it may be desirable to aim at. It contents itself with enlarging and strengthening the mental powers. It unrolls before the young man the ample page of knowledge, confident that this is the best preparation for any path that he may finally choose.

If, then, it is best for the young man that by a liberal education, his memory should be strengthened, his reasoning powers disciplined, his judgment matured, his mind enlarged—why is it not best for the young woman also? This is a question for those who differ with us to answer. It is a question that none would seriously ask, were it not that the minds of many are unconsciously swayed by a belief in the essential inferiority of woman. It can only arise from this pernicious error, or from some doubt as to the real advantage of a liberal education;—an error and a doubt, both of which should be remanded to the Dark Ages.

Generally, then, we would say, that there is no reason why woman should be debarred from any part of the studies common to all liberally educated men.

I say, common to all liberally educated men. I do not wish you to infer that I consider the course of instruction in our colleges for young men in every particular the wisest and the best. On the contrary, early in my college life I thought, and the years of maturer life have strengthened the idea, that in the curriculem of colleges, too little importance attaches to the science of nature, and to the study of the human soul,—not the study of the abstract metaphysics which the schoolmen bequeathed to us, but of man as he is,—and too little importance attaches to the study of the Hebrew and the Christian Scriptures,—the fountain whence the ever-enlarging river of our civilization flows. Neither did I then think, nor do I now think, that a familiarity with the classics alone, is either a sufficient, or altogether the best, preparation for life in our own day—for a life in which shall pulsate all the great emotions of our time, —for a life in complete sympathy with nature, with man, and with God.

In the United States, the college course for young men was modeled after that of the European Universities, which were founded when the Greek and the Latin were the only fully developed tongues; when the languages of modern Europe were in a formative process; when works on science, philosophy, medicine, jurisprudence, and theology, and all legal documents, state papers, and treaties, were done in Latin; when all discussions and correspondence were carried on in Latin; and when modern science yet waited for the thoughts of Bacon, the intuitions of Kepler, and the discoveries of Galileo.

Now, on the other hand, the Italian, French, German, and other languages, have been brought to a high state of perfection, and almost every work on art, science, literature, or philosophy, is composed in the author's vernacular. Yet our colleges, with unfortunate fidelity, have hitherto adhered much too closely to the course of study marked out by their ancient models.

But nothing should gratify the friends of education more than the changes that are now beginning to take place, not only in our own institutions of learning, but even in the English Universities of Oxford and Cambridge. The Novum Organum of Bacon has triumphed, and is leading us from the study of a dead Past to the study of living and eternal truth. The establishment of scientific departments and schools of mines, in connection with some of our noble and time-honored colleges and universities, is a virtual acknowledgment that not the ancient classics, but the modern classics, should rank first in the studies of youth; not the classics of the Greeks and Romans, but the classics of Nature.

I would not be misunderstood in this matter. The grand classics are grand indeed! Greece and Rome were grand; but their grandeur grew out of high aspirations, tending to a grand life. They turned neither to the right nor to the left, they looked not backward, they went right straight on, and thus became truly great.

We, too, have a greatness, as a nation, to attain: and we must attain it, if at all, in the same way. We need not fear that the truth developed by different nations, will or can be lost. Truth once known can never be hidden. The results of each generation and century, pass on into the future, and are interwoven into the woof of our ever-growing civilization.

The Greek and Roman energy, thought, and character, permeate the life and soul of modern Europe. The arts, the sciences, the literature, the civilization, of Greece and Rome we have to-day. They are out on the air; they are incorporated in our social and intellectual life; they are not afar off, they are here to-night—here in our streets, here in our homes and in our hearts. They are living, and speak with living tongues:—that part of them found in books alone may truly be called "dead."

In our opinion, a college founded to-day, should conform its curriculum to the growth of the world, in letters, and thought, and science, and civilization, and Christianity;—while the Greek and Latin languages should be studied only for specific ends.

If we had the years required for a thorough study of the classics, and an equal time to give to the natural sciences, then both might be pursued to advantage. But as we have not time to pursue to any considerable extent more than one of these departments, I would give a rudimentary training in the classics, and devote the best energies of the young to those studies which have for their objects, life and its pursuits, man and his destiny, God and His works.

The sphere of woman differs widely from that of man; but this is neither the time nor the place to unfold our views upon the question in what way, and to what extent, this fact should modify the course of study in a college for women; a question which all must recognize as one of great practical difficulty, as well as of great practical importance. The conclusions at which we have arrived on these subjects—the results in part of experience, and in part of the cordial aid of a large number of distinguished educators—will soon be laid before the public in the curriculum of the college.

We therefore here content ourselves with repeating, that generally the studies pursued by women should be those that are pursued by men; and that they should be pursued much to the same extent. Surely, there is nothing which the under-graduate learns in his college course, which he should not be glad that his wife should know as well as himself. Surely a liberal education has miserably failed of its aim, when a man desires in a wife, not an equal, but a toy or a slave.

The idea of woman as a slave is a barbarian idea. The savage has it to perfection, and because he has it he is a savage. The savage makes woman do the work of a beast of burden; the half-civilized Chinese puts on her all the drudgery of hard work;—"the wife drags the plough, the husband sows the grain."

To the savage, woman is a slave. The half-civilized man combines with this the idea of woman as a toy. This is an unchristian idea; unhappily it is too common even with us; yet, with some other degrading ideas, it is a relic of heathenism. The whole difference between civilized Europe, half-civilized Asia, and savage Africa, can be accurately measured by the idea of woman; the best test of civilization, in either a nation or an individual.

The question, then, whether our civilization is to advance or to retrograde—stand still it cannot—depends on the place hereafter to be given to woman. As to this question, the present seems to be a sort of crisis. The signs point both ways; on the whole, the prospect is hopeful and cheering: but we must either go back or go on; we must become either more Asiatic or more Christian.

The hopeful indications are general in their character, and embrace all that is cheering in the signs of the times. Those that forebode evil are more specific in their relations to women; and, though differing among themselves, they all point to one common end, viz., the destruction of the family.

The Church, the State, and the Family, are alike ordained of God. The ordering of the Family pertains to woman; of the State, to man; of the Church, to the Lord Jesus Christ. Each of these organizations exists by divine right, and therefore, within its own sphere, is sovereign. Yet the preservation and perfection of all, depend on that of each. In the words of a distinguished Greek scholar: "Each inculcating the same lesson, although with sanctions continually ascending; each successively, in the order of its rank, supplying the defects of the lower; yet each to be regarded as divinely appointed by the same eternal Source of all law and rightful authority, in heaven and earth."

The family is destroyed when its unity is destroyed. Of various causes tending to this result, we shall speak only of two particulars in our legislation. According to the law of Christ, the husband and wife are one person: to this fact, the old common law in a good degree conformed; but the tendency of recent statutes is to do away with this idea, by making the property of the wife distinct from that of the husband, and giving to her separately its management;—thus at once creating a diversity of interests.

We recognize the necessity, in certain cases, of such a distinction in the control of property: but we deplore this necessity, we are fearful as to its tendency, and we hope that the practice may never extend beyond rare and exceptional cases.

If each of the contracting parties, as they might properly be called, have large possessions, so that the disposal of property does not often arise, the evil is less. But with the great majority of families that compose the body-politic, the spending of a little of their very little money is a question of moment, that comes up from day to day, and almost from hour to hour: and if a garment cannot be bought, or a meal provided, without raising the question of separate pecuniary interests between the heads of the family, and that too in the presence of the children, the unity of the home, its sacred peace, and its hallowed lessons, are at an end; and it may be that the strong passions so constantly appealed to, will rend the family asunder. We have heard of a legacy of seven hundred dollars to a wife, that led to a divorce.

In accordance with the effect of such legislation, made to cover exceptional cases, but which is ominous of general corruption, are those laws of divorce which, in several of our States, practically tend to make marriage a contract dissoluble at the will of the parties; thus encouraging persons foolishly to rush into it, and madly to break from it. It is said that in one New England State, one marriage in ten is thus dissolved! The State thus presumes, for causes that the Church does not hold to be sufficient, to put assunder those whom God hath joined together.

Our object is by no means to discuss these subjects, but merely to glance at them as illustrations of a strong tendency to innovate without due regard to the sacred oneness of the family. Even education is an evil, so far as it may tend to infringe upon this unity; and it is of the highest value, only as it may tend to secure it. This is the true ground of the principle which we before laid down, and which we would extend to every grade of society, from the highest to the lowest, viz., that the wife should have as good an education as the husband; and, what is of equal importance, the mother should have as good an education as the children.

Whatever breaks in upon the oneness of the family, brings with it evil for which it cannot furnish any sufficient compensation, either to woman or to man. The destruction of the family is the destruction of woman: it is that of man also.

The destruction of the family is likewise the destruction of the State. The family is the foundation stone on which the higher edifice rests; and if this stone be removed out of its place, or ground to powder, the more imposing fabric of government falls to ruin. The no-family and no-government fallacies are the same in principle; and they complete themselves when they add, no Church, and no God.

The profligacy of our cities, like the poison of the cholera, infecting the whole of the country; the frenzy of fashion, bewildering the minds of women; the lust of gold, gnawing at the hearts of men; these things of themselves might lead us to fear that the family and the home might become things of the past; and if so, our civilization would vanish, "like the baseless fabric of a vision." But we look for better things: Christ, the Word of God, "by whom and for whom are all things," laid the foundations of the family so deep, that they cannot be removed. We may disregard them, to our destruction, as did Babylon and Rome of old, but whatsoever He hath decreed, He will finally bring it to pass.

That ideal of woman which we would fain behold realized, is His ideal. He ordained that the place of woman should be by the side of man, as his equal; and this ideal, which He foreshadowed in the Scriptures from the beginning, He will accomplish. His religion is a religion of far-continuing purposes; it is one religion, from the first promise that the seed of the woman should bruise the serpent's head, to the end of the world.

It may be an appropriate close to these somewhat discursive, yet related, remarks, to show that the idea of woman in the old Hebrew Scripture, was the germ that Christianity is ripening to the flower.

One book of the Scripture seems to have been written to place a Hebrew youth in full possession of all the wisdom of age. It states that its design is "to give to the young knowledge and discretion." I speak, of course, of the book of Proverbs. This is an extended series of practical precepts; of precepts everywhere marked by that religious sentiment which ever gives to practical truth its highest value; of precepts embracing the whole life of man; of precepts so profound and exhaustive, that the wisdom and the experience of all subsequent ages and nations have added to them but little.

From the difficulty of rendering axioms and pithy sayings into another language, our translation of this book is somewhat defective. It often misses the point of the saying which it aims to reproduce. But there can be no mistake as to the leading ideas in the description before us. The place that it holds in the book of all human wisdom, is good evidence that a high place was meant to be given to woman in the Hebrew Scripture; its opening and its closing words, moreover, strengthen this impression. The value of a perfect woman "is far above rubies." "The heart of her husband doth safely trust in her; he shall have no need of spoil." Precious gems—the favorite form of wealth among the Orientals—are thus disparaged in comparison with her; and he that hath a true woman, needs no other riches.

In the very spirit of the first divine word as to woman—"It is not good for man to be alone"—it is here written; "She shall do him good and not evil all the days of her life."

Again, at the close of the description, it is written, "Give her of the fruit of her hands"—that is, deal justly with her—yield not to the mean spirit, that thinks that whatever is conceded to woman, is so much taken from the birthright of man. The writer goes beyond the proverb of the French: "A good wife is half the battle;" and, though the husband is "known in the gates, when he sitteth among the elders of the land," his prosperity seems wholly attributed to her. Indeed, he is reduced to such insignificance, that all he can do is to stand still and praise her. This he does with hearty good will; saying, as good husbands always say to good wives—common excellence in woman always affecting a man with uncommon surprise—

"Many daughters have done virtuously, but thou excellest them all."

Young Ladies of the First Graduating Class of Rutgers Female College.

In this portraiture of a woman of another country and of a distant age, to which, for various reasons I have called the attention of the general audience, there are inwrought characteristics, the excellence of which I would, in this hour of parting, hold up to you for imitation.

"She worketh willingly:"—"in her tongue is the law of kindness:"—in her heart is the fear of the Lord.

Of the many things that I would gladly impress on your hearts, as I address you, as my pupils, for the last time, I can select but few, and perhaps none more appropriate than the virtues and excellencies which this portrait suggests.

One characteristic of this woman is energy: "She riseth while it is yet night":—"She eateth not the bread of idleness." She exemplifies the spirit of the truly Scriptural precept: "Whatsoever thy hand findeth to do, do it with thy might." Her example, then, is one of habitual industry, a habit which has much more to do with a truly virtuous life than is generally supposed. Labor strengthens all the virtues; idleness weakens them all:—idleness is the fruitful source of vice.

In every sphere in which you may be placed, there will be work to be done;—to be done religiously—that is, faithfully as unto God;—to be accepted by you as His manifest will, and to be done willingly as unto Him.

One of the chief ends of your education has been, to give you the trained intellect, that you may quickly and correctly discern, in each relation and circumstance of life—from day to day, and from hour to hour—what is the work that you are called upon to do. Another chief aim has been to give you that disciplined self-command that will enable you—not lazily putting it off till a more convenient season—to do it at once, and to do it thoroughly and well.

If you have here gained or strengthened the habit of industry, preserve it to the end. Without labor, there is no excellence and no happiness. It is the most vulgar of all vulgar errors, that a lady is a person who does nothing. Such a person would be good for nothing, and miserable indeed. Work, however, is of many kinds; work of the brain, and work of the heart, as well as work of the hands; and the humblest kind is not the hardest.

It is another vulgar error, that work is degrading. Labor was imposed on our fallen race, because it was fallen; but the decree went forth more in pity than in anger. Work was not imposed upon the angels, for they needed no such compulsion. Angelic natures work willingly and cheerfully; and how is the idea that to do nothing is a desirable thing, reconciled with the sublime words, "My Father worketh hitherto and I work."

In the description of the woman of old, it is said: "In her tongue, is the law of kindness;" and this I would most earnestly entreat you to emulate, believing that few things would conduce more to your usefulness and happiness. Saint James tells us that "if any man seemeth to be religious, and bridleth not his tongue, this man's religion is vain." Elsewhere in his Epistle, you may learn how difficult a thing he conceives this to be. It requires a perfect control of one's self, and a large charity. Of the former, we hope that you have gained something here; the other, you can gain somewhat from experience, but in perfection only from the grace of God.

I would have your conversation governed by the charity of which the Apostle Paul saith, that it "suffereth long and is kind; envieth not; vaunteth not itself; is not easily provoked; thinketh no evil." This kindness of spirit, this charity, is a high Christian grace; but it might almost be taught by experience, seeing how little we really know the motives that sway the human soul, and how often the severe judgments which we pronounce on our fellow-mortals, have to be reconsidered with much pain and self humiliation, when perhaps it is forever too late to right the wrong, and to recompense the suffering that we have occasioned.

Friendships broken, causeless enmities, opportunities for doing good and getting good thrown away, too often teach us—too late to prevent, to ourselves and to others, much lasting injury—the value of the law of kindness as the law of our words. Especially is this law of kindness needed in the speech of woman, whose hasty, thoughtless words can influence to fury the pride and wrath of man, and set on fire his heart with the fires of hell. Dissensions in families, hatred between neighbors, enmity between states and nations, follow when woman's tongue embitters man's jealousy and passion.

If the sphere of woman is hereafter to be enlarged, we all should more earnestly hope, and more fervently pray, that she may everywhere carry with her "the ornament of a meek and quiet spirit, which is in the sight of God of great price."

What is the characteristic in woman that should most fasten the affections, and secure the esteem, of man? Is it the varying charm of manner, or beauty of person? The Scripture before us, answers these questions in a few decisive words: "Favor is deceitful,"—that is, an unsatisfying thing

—"and beauty is vain; but a woman that feareth the Lord, she shall be praised."

I know few things, even in the Scripture, so thoroughly justified by observation, and at the same time so little known and regarded, as this. In the Hebrew Scriptures, the fear of God answers to the love of God in the Christian Scriptures, and so may be taken as equivalent to true piety: and true piety in woman is that alone which really can draw from out the heart of man, the sentiment of lasting veneration.

I cannot urge this as a motive for cultivating the spirit of piety; but I surely should not conceal from you what this Scripture so clearly reveals, in this: "Godliness hath the promise of the life that now is, as well as of that which is to come." But I would here enforce upon you the duty of piety, from other considerations. Piety is not only the highest of duties, but the greatest of privileges.

Young Ladies, life is so limited, our responsibilities are so great, the consequences of pursuing a wrong course are so terrible and destructive,—even so far as this life goes,—that you cannot afford to make a mistake at the outset. Experience is not always a sure guide—it cannot teach all the important truths that concern this life; nor can you trust implicitly to the wisdom of either parent or teacher, nor commit yourselves to the guidance of passion, or to the customs and opinions of the world. To what, then, should you go, to-night, to-morrow, and every day of your lives, for safe guidance—for true wisdom? Need I say, to the Bible alone?—to the Bible as opened to your minds, and brought home to your hearts, by the Holy Spirit granted to you in answer to prayer. By thus listening to its voice, you listen to the voice of God; by taking hold on its

truths, you take hold upon eternity. You are thus lifted above yourselves;—above your passions, your littleness, your ambition;—above the world. You are thus brought into communion with the Father of your spirits;—with God, who alone is sufficient to fill all the aspirations of the soul. He alone is wise enough to be your sufficient counsellor;—He alone is strong enough to give mortals strength.

Of His glory and His beauty, all the glory and the beauty of the things that He has made, are but faint emblems and reflected lights. He alone is worthy to be loved "with all your heart, and mind, and soul, and strength."

"Remember," then, "your Creator in the days of your youth." "The fashion of this world passeth away:"—"lay up for yourselves treasures in heaven, where neither moth nor rust doth corrupt." "Set your affections on things above, where Christ sitteth at the right hand of God": "and the very God of peace sanctify you wholly; and I pray God your whole spirit and soul and body be preserved blameless unto the coming of our Lord Jesus Christ."

www.ingramcontent.com/pod-product-compliance
Lightning Source LLC
LaVergne TN
LVHW020634110826
845149LV00004B/1189
9781418191139